MAN DOWNTOWN
& Other Short Stories

by Olivia Hill

First Paperback Edition

oliviahillwrites@gmail.com

www.oliviahillwrites.com

Table of Contents

ONE

Signs Remembered

The words are etched in planks of beautiful cedar, each board glistening with a honey brown finish. Opaque porcelain of green, blue, and red enamels pool in the carved words. "Two Rivers School and Recreation Area," the sign announces. An onyx arrow indicates the gravel path below.

Early in the day, clouds had wept mist on the road that ran between where I stood and where I was going. I walked across the tarred road and there I find another sign advertising the busiess and owner's name, Lindsey's Milling Co. It hangs there in its graceful age, no shame of its condition, proud of a job well done. It centers itself between two log columns and suspends from a railroad tie. The rusty chain holding the sign shrills when a wind comes along.

The carved words are still raised from the wood, but only slightly legible. There are no bright colors pooling in these weary etched words. It just hangs there, displaying itself in a manner that was once fashionable.

The wood's surface was left raw from a process called hewing which has taken its place in history. Rough, jagged edges were left on the surface as though to protect it from its only predators: those that made it. Blanched, weathered colors of mauve-gray and black prove the twenty-six years of occupation. Subtle tones and oils were lost to forty and fifty below temperatures, unseasonal rains and warm draining rays from the summer sun. I stand there watching the sign sway in the wind.

My nostrils open wide to take in the smells of lavender and wet, decomposing spruce. I feel only conscious of the sign and the smells. I know that the sign acts only as a cover to the novel, and the rest lay along the dusty path in front of me. I don't walk the path, deciding to leave it for another to explore.

TWO

Oh God Forgive Me for Thinking That!

The white church seemed lost beneath the previous night's snowfall, with only rolls of charcoal-black roofing paper and two-by-fours stretched across its top indicating the church's existence. The smell of our cargo permeated the car with clove, pumpkin, cinnamon, nutmeg, and apples. Carefully we organized the transferring of five pies, one sheet cake, four loves of stuffed bread, and a Coleman cooler with the makings for punch. The feeling of importance and sinful pride molded my mind. I thought of how I was probably the only one who brought so much food, and everyone would surely be grateful for each delicious morsel.

We walked into the unfinished fellowship room. The walls were only partially painted, and the floors were without carpet or rugs. A couple of the brothers moved about in a small cubical which was to be the kitchen. They rushed about the room trying to install a stove, the kind that is used in big commercial establishments. High-backed, long seats resembling those out of a school bus were pulled up to makeshift tables of plywood stationed on wooden horses. Red and green crepe paper was draped over the table to make the humble setting more formal. We set the food on the table next to oddly shaped dishes, with foil holding their contents. Clear plastic wrap covered the

dishes I brought in, allowing the golden-brown crusts of my pies and creamy white icing with sugared violets to show through.

Maybe whatever is under that foil should stay under the foil. (Oh God, forgive me for thinking that way).

Boomp, boomp went the pedal striking the drum. "Oh, thank you, Lord," an occasional voice spouted from a saint's mouth. These voices rose up around my ears, coupled like flesh mating with sounds from the bass guitar, drum and spirit-lifted feet that shook the floorboards beneath me. Two other women stood around fumbling with dishes from one hand to another, to one table to the other, trying to look in charge. I too stood there stalling, not wanting to go into Sunday's service, acting like a kid who got a special privilege in class, then stalls to keep from going back.

Another member of the church walked in with a couple of dishes. She's a new member. I had eyeballed her earlier and made the decision that she acted funny-- kind of stuck on herself. I looked her over and smiled politely when our eyes met.

"Do you need any help?" She said in no particular direction.

"No," the reply came back from one of the ladies acting in charge.

But she just stood there like the rest of us. *Why don't she leave*, I thought. *(Oh God, forgive me for thinking that.)*

The music in the sanctuary rose louder with the shouts of, "Thank you, Jesus, oh wonderful savior". Then a scream that pierced the wall woke all of us from our thumb-twiddling. The two women that were supposed to be in charge trotted across the floor, spiked heels on, and smiles slapped across their faces.

"Ooowee, they sound like they're having a good time in there," one of the sisters said, sticking her head through the door. Then they entered where the rest of the congregation was clapping their hands and jumping with a hopscotch step to their stride. I decided to make the punch. I was pleased that the position of supervisor had opened up and any decision to be made was mine. I could walk right into the position without any competition from the remaining sister. She had arrived after me and would have no idea if I was the one appointed to be in charge from the start. Opening the apple juice cans, then filling them from my only source of water, the restroom sink, I strutted across the floor with quick steps like the survival of the world depended on me reaching the cooler.

"Can I help you?" The remaining sister asked.

Damn, I thought. *(Oh forgive me for thinking that.)* "Ah, well, if you want, you can get the water," I said.

She moved back and forth from the sink filling the cooler. Between each refill, we talked. Then some small nothing, like wasting water, would evoke Deja vu. We laughed at the amusing little stories we thought of. Before the return of the other two sisters, we had made a punch and laughed about Southern mommas and their good cooking. We cut six pies and talked about getting your socks knocked off by those same mommas. Sliced two sheet cakes and giggled about funny-looking black men who didn't deserve any mommas. Cut four loves of stuffed bread and chuckled about how funny most black people are about eating something if it didn't look like big momma's cooking.

The two sisters came back. They looked as satisfied in their activities as we were in ours. Their cocoa-brown faces with a three-shade difference between them were warm and sweaty looking, like the faces of early morning joggers. Looking around briefly and with a half-hearted desire to be back in this area of the church, they left again, returning to the song, 'I'm not afraid of the gospel of Jesus Christ,' being bellowed by Sister Jackson and the choir. Her voice rang like an angel laid back enjoying sweet milk and buttered cornbread. We screwed around a few more minutes, then slipped in.

The church was packed. We slid along to one side passing full pews of saints jumping and shouting on each end. Reaching the back, we found no seats left, so we stood between the wall and the last pew. The smell of sweat condensed between the broken plastered walls reminded me of the lingering odor of sweet lovemaking without the sweet parts. The extra layers of fat left from my pregnancy fried like fat bacon in a black skillet from the heat coming off the exposed copper pipe that ran along the wall behind me. In perfect view of the whole church with the other sister next to me, we joined in clapping and praising the Lord with uplifted hands and faces waiting for the power of the Holy Ghost to touch us. "Thank you, Jesus...*slap, stamp, slap, stamp*...hallelujah, hallelujah, hallelujah, thank God, thank God! We're here today to magnify the lord! Our wonderful savior!" *Slap, stamp*...!

The voice of evangelist Walker rose to the pitch of a small Gabriel blowing his horn with the rhythm of the whole congregation's feet and hands to back her up. The organ cranked up winning and grinning like a giddy drunk doing a jig on one foot but intoxicated with the spirit of God.

Some started to run down the aisle wavin' their arms like a flightless bird. Then someone got a dance, feet movin' fast as a hummingbird's wings. Then another gotta dance. She started shakin' like ice-water had been poured on her. Then she began to hop up and down on one foot in the middle of the aisle wipin' and wrappin' herself with long bony arms trying to wring the ice water out. Our heads became woozy from this ancestral beat. "Oh Lord, give me the Holy Ghost too," I thought. The spirit moved through the church. The deacons, elders, and just brothers shook the floor with Watusi jumps.

The spirit died down to a low flicker in its victims, leaving them only enough strength to flex their nostrils for a shot of warm air.

I looked around at the white visitors trying to cut through the dense humidity of body heat with European noses. I smirked to myself and hoped that these white descendants of Europe might feel some of what it was to be in the hot hull of a slave ship flesh to flesh. *(Oh God!)*

The pastor stepped up to the pulpit and said, "Do you all feel alright? Raise your hands if you feel alright." Everyone raised their hands. "I'm not going to hold you any longer. I want to thank the visitors for coming out and invite them to come again. Would the visitors go on into the fellowship room first? One of the ushers take them on in. Now the church is dismissed. We can eat." Everyone stood and a dark cloud moved from the pews like a small stampede and went through the door to the food. Two white faces showed up to eat out of the six that sweated through the service. One of them stood back waiting for some direction. I laughed to myself again and thought, *Poor thing, he'll starve to death if he don't get in there and nudge and bump elbows with these folks. Oh Lord, forgive them for their stomachs being bigger than their manners.*

"Come on up here this way, brother, and grab you a plate," I said.

I took two plates and fed my daughter and husband and then helped serve and heat food. One by one, the serving women disappeared with plates filled with food. I ran around trying to keep food hot in the microwaves and clearing away empty dishes.

Carrying a large dish of meat, I held it while looking for a place to set it. Before I could find a spot, one of the sisters rushed up to me and said, "Where're you going with that meat? Give me some of that!" and started sticking the meat with her fork. I stood there and gave her a dirty look and thought, *I hope you drop some right on them purple shoes. (Oh Lord, I just...kinda mean that!)* She glanced at my eyes and sheepishly got the message. After that, I decided to fix my own plate.

An hour passed and all who had brought food were about the only ones left waiting for their dishes. We started packing up what was left of the food we brought. The pastor thanked everyone and then asked politely if someone would fix him a plate. "Whatever is left, daughter, will be fine," he said to one of the sisters standing behind the table. The thin-framed man sat quietly eating with a shine in his 80-year-old eyes. I thought to myself, *Oh thank you, Lord, for grace.*

THREE

Mama Takin' Me Downtown

Mama takin' me downtown today. She never took me there before. She always say, "No reason to drag no colored chil' round proper white folks where she don' belong," But today I'm ten and Daddy, that no-count whoochie-coochie man (that what I hear Mama callin' him sometimes when she sittin' on the pot, talking to herself), he give her some money and some extra for my birthday. He said take me downtown and get me something nice, like them white folks' kids she work for got. Mama just looked at Daddy and say, "Don't be tellin' me how to spen' these few pennies." Later she say to me it ain't enough to pay no bills no how and mites well get me somethin', cause I'm lookin' raggedy as felark.

We got the streetcar and walkway in back. I scared at first when it start to move, so I move in close to Mama. She nudge me back over and whisper for me to set up straight. There ain't but five other peoples and the rest white. There was a black man that sat next to me in another chair. He kinda look like my daddy. They both real dark, black-red, have big white teefs like a horse, and black wavy hairs with lots of conk on it. He spoke, but I don't member what he said cause I was scared still. But I member he spoke nice like the sound of a drum outside floatin' on the air.

When the streetcar finally stop, Mama and me got off and walk down the sidewalk. It a gray color and real clean. I's can see tiny rocks shining in it like gold. I think--these peoples rich if they got gold to walk on. I try not to step on they's gold but too many to miss and Mama jerkin' my hand and saying walk like I got some sense.

There were lots of white folk and black folk too. Mama would nod when we pass someone white and step aside when there weren't enough room for us to pass. I saw all kind of tall buildings, cars and people eatin' in front of big glass windows where everybody outside can sees them and they can sees us when they takin' a break from chewin'. Mama tell me don't be starin'. Ain't proper.

Mama and me walk to the end of the earth, I think. We stop at a shop made of brick with a lit'le glass window that had a dummy in an old long, gray dress; but it had no head.

Mom spoke to a woman with skin the color of the vanilla paper and pointy eyes that go up. I know she Chinese or somethin' cause we learnt about them in school. She look like my oldest sister kinda, cause my oldest sister got squidy eyes like that, and yellow-like skin, her and Mama does. When I ask Mama how come she got eyes and skin like that she say cause somebody was messin' in the wood pile way back. Mama, the lady and I went up and down rows of cloth that smell like old and spice, too. Then they stop at a rack with clothes that would fit me. Mama and the lady went through pullin' out stuff and fittin' it to my back, then puttin' it back and doin' it all over again. Mama would yell, "Stand up straight!" and then almost knock me over fittin' somethin' to me. Mama finally took out a dress. It was white with a big red bow and lots of tiny color circles; red, yellow, brown, that just touch each other and made a new color. Mama put the dress up to me, then pull it down and said, "This to big too." I turn roun' fast an almos' said somethin', anythin'. Mama frowned, so I didn't. She look a little longer, then pick up the dress again and said, "You want it. I guess I can take it in till you grow into it."

We went back the same way and stood in front of the store to wait for the streetcar. The store window had a girl dummy in a white dress with light pink, yellow flowers, and green stems. There was a lady dummy too in a white ruffled dress with large purple flowers and green and brown stems. A tall lady, she had dark brown hair, had walk up to the window holdin' the hand of a girl my age that jump up and down a lot. The lady remind me of my Aunt Sara, she that tall, too, and got that kinda brown hair. Mama smile and step a little over to one side so the lady could see in the window good and we could stay in the shade. The girl didn't have brown hair like the woman. She had yellow hair. So I thought maybe that wasn't her mama until she said it. She look at me and roll her brown eyes then she started hoppin' up and down again saying, "Mother buy me that dress! I want that dress!"

I think that's how she said it.

Her mama look down at her and said, "Ok, but stop your hoppin'."

The girl and the woman turn to go in the store. She turns back to me and whispers, "You black nigger." Then start hoppin' again. The streetcar came. I look up at mama. She took my hand and smiled without lookin' at me. We got on the streetcar and sat down closer to the front 'cause there weren't a lot of white people sittin' there.

I thought, "I don't look like what she said." I look in my brown paper bag at my dress and think, "I look like this," and then I sat up straight without Mama even tellin' me.

FOUR

Just Like a Man

It was well into October and deer season was a month away. The earth was like an old arthritic woman, and unable to protect her spoils. The men, who had sat all year down at Jimmy's bar in personalized seats, were now in their garages wiping down the long barrow of an ought-six, waiting for the sacred rite of man. The young men in rebellion, drove half-painted pickup trucks fast around town. With beer in hand, they spun trucks in circles, making donuts on the dirt roads while the gravel sprayed in refute to fall. The wind blew every ten minutes, swirling leaves into a ring around the rosy dance. Closed coal-iron plants sat like haunted houses, yet the memory of billowing smoke revisited the nostrils of townspeople that happened to pass by. These smells were reserved for Mansville steel-bred people. And their inheritance was the belching up of smoke from singed lungs.

Mave Donkelish hustled down the main street with a bag of groceries in her arms. A red and white speckled scarf held back her dark brown, permed hair and a hello slipped from her lips when passing someone. Payday visited her hand and then went on its way after stopping at the grocers and creditors before she could get home. It was already six. Her stride quickened home to put supper on the table for her husband and three-year-old son. She reached her yellow pickup and placed the bag in the rusting metal bed. A softened, tinny voice from behind her made her jump to attention.

"Oh, it's you Mary Lynn. You scared me."

"Well, good! I've been trying to reach you since last week and you ain't returned a call yet, Miss Busy." said Mary Lynn, a delicate-acting woman of twenty-eight with soft, baby doll features that were over-made and frosted-tipped ends to her hair.

"Don't you start too."

"How y'all been?"

"Alright, I guess, you and John?"

"We gettin' out of here in two days. Goin' down to Oklahoma where my folks are. John don't like it but he can help on the farm--since my dad's on his back and you know I can't work--because that would really kill him."

Mave looked straight into Mary Lynn's eyes, then stepped up into the cab of the truck and slammed the door. Jarred by the sound, Mary Lynn realized her mistake and shifted the flaw to John.

"Mave, I didn't mean there's something wrong with a woman workin'. You know, John's old fashion."

"So is Canon, but we got bills and he won't try for a job in town…"

"Oh hell, it's six-thirty. I got to go. He'll be madder than shit."

Mave backed out fighting the steering wheel with muscles that rippled into a hump. Mary Lynn yelled after her that John and her were planning to come by later. She nodded approvingly and went bobbing up and down in the cab towards home.

She rushed in the door, bumping it closed with her wide hips that hung from a tiny needle-point hoop waist. The table is covered with morning dishes and a fresh layer of crumbs, milk, and coffee spills along with what looked like peanut butter, mayo, tuna, pork & beans, dried like glue to the vinyl tablecloth. She could hear the T.V. going in the living room. She set the bag in a chair and moved to the doorway separating the kitchen and front room and said, "Hi!" Trying to pick up her naturally flat voice, "Where's Lincoln? Y'all eat already--I brought some burgers for dinner." She leaned against the door frame with one foot bent up.

"Yeah, we ate," said Canon. "Where you been?"

"I told you I went to the store. There's beer, too, you want one." She turned slightly in motion to get him one.

"What this look like, a bottle of mouthwash?" He lifted the can just at the wrist to make notice of it. Canon yelled from the living room.

"Lincoln, your mama's home."

A little face appeared around the corner in the same doorway she'd just stood in. Lincoln rocked on his heels making his shoulders move back and forth while he looking at the ground facing the kitchen.

"Come here. Don't you have a kiss for me, Lincoln?" She squatted down with her arms open. He sombered over and threw his arms around her neck.

"What's wrong, you get in trouble?"

Then Canon's voice said he sure did. "I told him to go to the can. He wouldn't and he peed himself--so he goes to bed early tonight. Right, partner?" Canon looked down with a slight grimace and thick bushy eyebrows made into one; raised in the center. Mave tried to console Lincoln as much as possible without stepping on toes.

"You're a big boy Lincoln and accidents happen but your daddy told you to go potty, didn't he?

"Yes," Lincoln said, a sob caught in his voice.

"Well, since you've eaten already there's some ice cream in the bag. You can have a bowl before bed." His face brightened. She went over and got a dish from the cabinet, pulled the ice cream out--plain vanilla-- dished up a bowl and sent him to his room.

"I saw Mary Lynn. She said they're coming by later."

Canon enters and stands in the doorway. "Yeah, I saw John down at Jimmy's earlier. The bum is going to live with his in-laws. Can you believe that?" He looked at her not really for a response but was about to get one when he said, "You can forget it! I'm a steel man, my father was, my brothers and grandfather, and if they believe this country couldn't do without the plants then so do I. They hung in through worse times than these."

"I wasn't going to say that."

"Yeah, you were thinkin' it."

Mave never replied. She had run a sink full of hot water. She stuck her hands in and swished around the cloth. Her hands ached from the heat forcing them to warm; it felt good, almost orgasmic. She stood there immersed for a moment, then took the cloth and began to scrub the table. He stood, perched against the refrigerator, turning up the last of the beer to his mouth but keeping his eyes on the rear end that bent in front of him, controlled by the person scrubbing the vinyl tablecloth. He walked up to her and, with two hands grabbed her at the creases of her bend, leaned over and whispered in her ear an invitation to get a little before their company came, and then he pinched the points her thighs and buttocks made.

"Damn it Canon, that hurt. What's the matter with you."

The back door opened and the tinny voice that made her jump to attention before did it again.

"What you doing to that girl, Canon." Mary Lynn's voice rang out. Mave turned to face her. "Ain't that just like a man, see you busy and want to mess around."

John came in behind her.

"Y'all like it. Hey Canon, what you know. Got another brew?"

Canon laughed out loud. "Come on in, man." He dug down into the refrigerator and pulled out a domestic beer, opened it, and tossed it to him laughing as John, a tall, wide, muscular man, juggled the beer upright and tried to suck the foaming suds spewing from the can.

"You're nuts," John said.

"You guys act like kids." Mary Lynn chided. Mave never said a word. Her face was placid and unsurprised. The men went into the living room while Mary Lynn engaged in hearing herself talk as Mave went about cleaning. The walls in the kitchen were grease-soaked and one side had been stripped for painting but had not been tended to since its stripper, Canon, was jobless. The sink was an old porcelain double basin that bled a dark navy color through. There was an old refrigerator that had to be thawed from a build-up of ice, and wooden cupboards with small glass windows. Mary Lynn rested her vocal cords to take a swallow of beer, and Mave could hear the men talking in the other room.

"I can't believe it," Canon said, "They talked you into it. What the hell are you going to do on a farm, slop hogs?"

"Listen, the old man has his foot in the grave and I got three kids to feed. What else am I gonna do? I can't work a city job. I don't know nothin' else but the steel mill." John spoke with a defeated tone.

"I know, but the mill's gonna start up again. This is temporary."

"Well, you make damn sure, buddy, you let me know. I'll be back for my shift the first day with some of them pigs I've been slopping between two slices of bread." They kicked up boots and muddy white socks in laughter, burping in rhythm.

"So it looks like you gonna miss hunting with me this year."

"Yeah, ain't that a pair of dirty drawers. Who you takin' with you?"

"You crazy, you think I want one of those fools getting me with a sound shot. No thanks. Plus, I don't want everyone to know my spots--you'll be back."

"You think they couldn't live without each other," Mary Lynn said. "What y'all talkin' about killin' them poor things for, they so cute. What's a sound shot anyway?" Mary Lynn asked, then waited for an answer to her question but one wasn't returned. On the contrary, barking for more beer was their only reply. Mary Lynn sat there as if she was still expecting an answer any minute.

Mave stopping her domestics and answered her with a little more expression. "It's when an inexperienced hunter shoots at the first sound he hears, and that could be an animal or you," John's voice rang out from the other room.

"Sounds like you got your hunter in there. You been teaching the little lady."

"No, little Miss Working Woman used to go hunting with her father when she was a kid."

"So why don't you take her with you?"

"I ain't taking no woman hunting with me." Canon burped in his mouth. The sour gas permeated with his words. He frowned and continued. "You know it just ain't in a woman to hunt, plus she told me the last time she and her father went, she got sick and threw up at the kill. Anyways I don't want her gettin' the idea she can start wearing the pants around here."

"What's the matter, wearin' an apron don't suit your taste?" John chuckled while Canon sat staring past nothing. "Ahh! Come on, I was just kiddin'. Lots of men's wives work." He said with a smirk, turning up the can and guzzling it.

Mave came in and sat two beers on the table, then went down the hall towards a light in a back bedroom. The soft sound of talking to a child filled the now-quiet rooms. Giggles came from the voice of not only a child but from a woman whose face and speech were otherwise veiled and monotone.

"Go and brush your teeth and I'll bring your jams in," the elated voice said. A few minutes passed, then the sing-song sounds of a story filled the house. A light was clicked off. Mave appeared back down the hall, changing her chameleon face back to a pasty-flesh color. Everyone was now sitting, listening to Mary Lynn and T.V. Mave sat down on the arm of Canon's chair and she broke the silence by asking what kind of farm Mary Lynn's parents had. The conversation continued as small talk but was taken over by Mary Lynn and John talking about town gossip and hunting gear. Mave settled into her usual stoic and silent demeanor while Canon took on a rather unusual presence. He was quiet.

John prodded "Come on man, you still pissed about what I said?"

"I ain't pissed," he said in a tone contrary to his expression. He lightened his voice and gave a half-drunk and sinister laugh. He reached his arm around Mave and jerked her back into his lap. She bobbed forward and hit the end table, sending five beer cans tumbling to the floor. A few of the cans cried a whining sound as they spun on the floor before stopping. With a reaction as if electrocuted, Mary Lynn's pale hands with press-on nails, colored malibu pink reached towards Mave and the crashing cans simultaneously. Mary Lynn's attempt to rescue Mave or the cans were useless. Almost instantly she recoiled, grimaced, and tried to position herself back into a doll-like composure. Mary Lynn shifted in her seat then pulled back her hair while clearing her throat as if she created the embarrassment. John sat mostly undisturbed with the exception of moving forward with his elbows that now rested on his knees and the swaying of his head methodically from side to side. When the last can on the ground finished its tone, John picked up the can and pressed the thin metal in and out making it pop to a plink, plink sound.

"Na, I ain't mad, just thinking 'bout what you said." He squeezed Mave and kissed her on the cheek. She pulled herself upright on his lap and started to get up. His arms tightened.

"Come on Canon, let go. We got company," she said, pressing lightly on his chest giving what would have been a smile on any other face.

He held her there and nibbled at her ear, then said loudly in her ear, "John here thinks I should take you hunting with me. How about it, honey?" She gave an expression like a deer frozen in headlights.

She pushed his arms away and climbed back to her perch on the arm of his chair and said, "You know I don't like hunting."

"Oh, that's right, I just thought you might want to try and be my partner for once, in hunting that is. But I forget you've been to college and learned that killing's bad."

"Mave, I didn't know you were in college, what did you take up?" Mary Lynn asked.

"I tried it for a little while, nothing to tell. I didn't go all the way through."

"She quit to hand out papers for green peas--you know, saving animals and stuff," Canon said with his eyes dancing about and lips lacquered in beer.

"Green peas?" In harmony, the couple asked.

"It's called GreenPeace--an organization to stop the killing of whales."

"Hey honey, I'm in danger of dying of thirst. Get me another beer." Canon falls back laughing, then speaks. "You want one, Johnny boy--get John another one?"

"Naw, I still got some."

Mave stood but hesitated and looked at him with questioning eyes.

"Come on, this is my last one--you know I ain't going to see John for a while. This will be to toast him."

She went into the kitchen without a word. He looked her over.   Her thighs, firm and meaty, her steps sure-footed as she walked into the kitchen. Canon leaned over the arm of his chair but slipped and missed placing his elbow. His head slid off his hand and landed one inch from hitting the elbow's intended place.

"Watch this. I know how to get her to go huntin'."

"Canon, why don't you leave it alone? You said it makes her sick," John said with empathy for the situation.

"It's time she sees what real men do. Because I ain't workin' doesn't mean I don't know how to be a man. Shh, you'll see…"

"Thanks, honey," Canon said. "I was just saying how nice it would be to have some fresh deer meat on the table. How it would really help out since I ain't able to work right now. I really would like your help. You don't have to shoot, just be the driver." She sat there with no reply. "I was telling Johnny the last time you went hunting with your father you got sick at the kill. I forgot to tell them why." Mave snapped her head towards him, then froze waiting for a movement or sound to see if it meant danger. He looked at her and smiled with a crooked mouth.

"Well, you see she was thirteen, been hunting with him since she was eight. The day he killed the doe--

did I say it was a doe, she wasn't supposed to go. She had followed in the woods when the shot went off. When she got to the place her father was…"

"Cut it out, Canon."

"Come on honey, they're friends. We can tell them," Canon said with a thread of victory.

John said, "Listen buddy, I'll give you a call before we get on the road."

"Yeah, you ass, I'm going to miss you. Listen, we'll bag one for you. Right, honey?" He stood and pulled her to his waist. The men shook hands, the woman hugged and promised to call one another, then the couple left. Mave began cleaning up the mess of cans. Suddenly, Canon grabbed her by the arm, took the can she was still holding and dropped it to the floor, pulling her up to him. "Hey, come on, you know I didn't mean anything, I was just messin' around-- they knew that, I just had a little too much to drink." He said, staring into her eyes. She stared back searching for him. "I need you to go with me hunting, do this for me! Ain't it enough that I can't work. My best friend is bailing on me, can't or won't go hunting. What happened was a long time ago, I want to show you real hunting---just let me be a man!" Mave said nothing and just nodded okay and slipped her hand from his to pick up the cans on the floor.

....

Two weeks later, the truck was filled with camping and hunting equipment. Their son was dropped off to family. Canon yelled from the driver's seat to Mave. "Come on!" He was used to leaving in the dark.

"Come on Mave. I want to get there before dark and set up."

She came out in her usual manner, dressed in a thick green sweater with a wool-lined dark vest and blue jeans. He glanced over at her with a half-approving look, and off they went.

They climbed a narrow dirt road into the Allegheny Mountains. Several years of leaves made a thick mulch on the path. Bright orange flat-topped toadstools relished in the molding mesh. The truck spun at Canon's persistence for it to climb. He then cranked it left so the truck sat diagonal to the path. Mave sat quietly, gripping the dash, not out of fear, but out of securing herself to the seat.

"I spotted this place the last time John and I went hunting. There's an old utility shack or something a mile or so up. We got an hour and half before dark. We'll walk in a mile or so. There's a clearing and a stream running down. We can camp down from that." Mave, without a word, fitted her pack on and helped with the other supplies.

"One thing I can't complain about is you talking too much." He laughed and she smiled.

"Here, you carry the Winchester." He pitched it over to her. She caught it and held it with a touch of hot metal. "Don't worry, I ain't asking you to shoot; just carry it just in case." Canon led the way, they trudged through a new bed of leaves. The wind blew puffs of air over naked trees. Clumps of aspens, oaks, and maples bared their bosoms in the canopy above their heads. Canon's feet fell heavily to the ground and sent red, gold, and brown leaves flying and all its nesting creatures pressed to the surface. He carried his gun with two hands across his chest in a military manner, eyes looking straight in front only taking in the peripheries of the land while his inner eye arranged the setting for a kill. Mave walked quietly behind barely disturbing the surface, with little effort, but with a fluidity, mimicking the leaves falling from the trees. She was here like the mushrooms that pushed through the mulch, and a deer foraging for food; she could have gone just as unnoticed. Her dark hair and eyes would make one expect a darker hue in the color of her skin but at home, she bared mostly a pale white lifeless color. But possibly it was the brisk walking, crispiness in the air, or remembered connection to nature that caused her face and neck to turn a peach-stone brown and cheeks circled, currant berry red. They had walked a mile without a word. The sky had dimmed to a gray-blue light. Then Canon, waking from his daydream, jolted to a sense of gallantry. He whirled around in concern that he lost her in his quick steps and spun calling her name.

"Mave."

She froze and he flinched, seeing she was only two yards away.

"Jesus, girl, I thought I lost you. How can you be so quiet?"

"I wasn't trying to be."

He turned back around and continued. Sweat formed at his brow. He wiped it with the back of his hand. He picked up his stride again, but his eyes glanced around occasionally, trying to keep her in view. The incident made him feel uneasy, superstitious. He had never felt uneasy before with her, although others had expressed discomfort because of her lack of social ability. He knew she wasn't a talker when he met her four years ago and that suited him fine. So, her quiet, withdrawn ways went mostly overlooked until now. Maybe it was having her here in a place that seemed strangely like her-- maybe that was the thing that made it eerie being with a person that seemed so perfectly suited for the place. He continued to look around at her more frequently. Her medium-stout body seemed more graceful than he'd seen before. She bled into the surroundings--she was beautiful. His penis hardened. He couldn't wait to set up camp.

They reached the area just above the creek. He pointed towards a tree line and said they would stay there. There was a clearing above the trees and only four yards from water. The light in the sky was less than an hour from being all together gone. They busied themselves setting up. When all was done, tent set, fire going, extra wood gathered, food smelling, and beer in Canon's hand, the night was well in. He spoke to her about the next day and what he wanted her to do. The one thing he stressed over and over again was she would have to carry a gun just in case of a bear, but whatever she did, make sure she knew what she was shooting at. The plan was for her to walk in, then back towards him making noise to drive prospective deer to him. He would be stationed in a spot, ready to make the kill. This was called *driving*. She reassured him she had no intention of shooting the gun and if she had to, she would know what it was that she was shooting at. They bedded down, the fire nearly flickered out and the sounds of its popping found the sounds of crickets and whippoorwills in an off-beat tune as he slid down into her sleeping bag, glowing at the shoulders, cream white.

....

Daybreak came and the sun was still low, working to crest the earth's surface. Canon awoke, rubbed his eyes, and stuck his head out of the pup tent. Mave was up and sitting next to the fire and sticking the coal, completely dressed. She poured a tin of coffee and held it out for him. He frowned and pulled back inside to dress. She hadn't thought he might expect or wanted to get up before her, but when he came out of the tent, walked over aways and urinated, then walked to the fire without a word, she knew he was wounded. "Those crickets kept me up most of the night.' Mave said. He looked over at her. "I guess I was just nervous about today, I woke early." The tension in his face smoothed and his tone softened when he spoke.

"Least I didn't have to wake you up, but I hope this isn't gonna mean you're given out on me today." She smiled and blew a frosty breath over her coffee.

They broke camp, snuffing out the last coals, and stashed away leftover food in a tree. Walking a ways towards the brook, he pointed to where she was to start her movement. In a low octave as if the deer were leaning over his shoulder, he said he thought deer probably used this brook but between last night and early morning, the deer caught their scent. He told her to circle around deep and long--going in at least a mile--then come down towards the brook, and he'll be waiting. After sweeping his hand across the land in front of them like some mighty creator, he pushed the thirty-ought-six to her, then questioned her as to whether she could handle it. She said yes and assured him it was nothing for her to walk and make noise. But they both chuckled at the idea of her making noise.

He pointed out to her that he would be stationed a bit up the hill on the other side of the brook and to remember he was there, and she was not to shoot unless necessary. He slow-jogged across the brook while she strode to her right. The sun had crested the hill and started heating the chilled air that Mave's breath only made mini-clouds in. After she walked for thirty minutes, she stopped and looked about the ground. Finding two large sticks with brotherly weight, she looked up at the sources from where the sun rays came. With eyes closed, in a prayer expression, she threw the thirty-ought-six over her shoulder to dangle on her back and started her walk again, whaling the two sticks together as she hooted and howled sounds of an animal unknown to the area. She pushed her way through her plotted path, while the occasional squirrel sent out chuckles of protest. A rabbit or two skidded away, and the forest bandit looked on at a lengthy distance with curiosity. The sun was now in full bloom, and the day promised to be a bright Christian Sunday.

She thought about the excuse she made this morning and how it was partly true. That she had been awake most of the night but not from crickets or fear of the next day. At least not from what he thought she was afraid of. Instead, she lay awake fearing something potentially good could turn bad once again. Memories of her childhood flooded in. How she used to rush to bed in the anticipation of waking early to go hunting with her father. Mave was an only child and the possibility of her playing dress-up with dolls and tea parties was made nearly impossible due to the bond she shared with her father. Mave became more of a wife to her father, after he lost his farm and cared for a wife who became invalid when Mave was ten. Now Mave was faced with her husband's loss of the steel mill and the weight of what that meant to her. Everything seemed so much more clearer standing out there in the woods. It had been years, but it all came back to her. Thoughts of the day she shot her first rabbit at nine, rushed in the smells, sounds, and every detail of that day. "Okay Mave," her father said. "You wait behind these bushes and when I scare something out, you hold the gun like I showed you and squeeze, easy."

"Alright, Daddy. I'm going to get one this time. You'll see," she replied with her young face beaming in the sun's rays and a crown of dark hair circling her face. She could see them all over again, with herself crunched down behind a bush praying for that rabbit to show her father. Her father was a big man and the cliché 'strong silent type' had him in mind. His fingers, she remembered, were wide as a broomstick. They both shared dark hair, hunting, and the same bloodline. He was old-fashioned and believed women could or should do only certain things. But after trying for so many years to get a son and only getting Mave, he mellowed, and hunting with her was the result.

Mave suddenly woke from her daydream and realized she had stopped banging and making her mangled animal cries. Mave had walked for several minutes with little attention to the direction she'd gone in and where she was exactly and turning wildly in a circle, confusing matters more. Then she stopped spinning, took a breath, and regained the serene stature she was known for. Looking around at the trees would do her no good since the trees were the same, and if there had been an unusual tree trunk or arrangement it was no use now due to her not paying any attention. She looked at her watch. Only fifteen minutes had passed so maybe she'd only walked a little over half a mile, which was good because that put her about where she should be. Then she looked at the ground for tracks, but the leaves were loose on the surface and the scattering of the leaves her feet made only added to a disorganized scene. Then a thought, possibly something said to her by her father in a similar situation or something just innate, but she looked up and towards the sun. It rose to the west, and she had walked into its eye. So now she knew she needed to turn and walk in a half-mile, then circle back towards the brook.

Mave made the circle and was several yards from the brook and above the spot where Canon sat waiting. She had stopped making noise a little ways back and had now moved in quietly to the position she took by an old elm tree, close to Canon. The day had come through just as foreseen, even more beautiful. The brook ran three feet from the grass embankment, with two large rocks stacked one on the other, giving the impression of a big man looking. Old driftwood laying around the large rocks gave the impression that the stone man had arms. Varied-sized rocks made a line in front of the stone man. The rocks set as somber parishioners waiting for a morning sermon. More stones stretched out in this congregational scene, past the shallow rocky brook into darker waters. The wind sent its hot breath to push the stained-colored leaves scampering about the cathedral as the heat kissed air also reclaimed the morning dew and the sweat of her brow.

Canon looked up at her with disappointment in his eyes, but without a word. Maybe the disappointing look was for the fact that nothing moved toward him for which she was responsible, or merely because he waited in a spot, he calculated there were to be deer and there were none. Nothing but this damn beautiful day. All was quiet for a moment. They waited as if not really waiting for anything, but just not ready to move or talk.

Canon rustled a few limbs of a bush, rising from the spot where he had sat quietly for almost two hours. Mave's eyes enlarged from a sudden movement she heard. He stopped the action of his muscles, looked into Mave's frozen eyes where she sat by the elm tree, almost unseen. She stared out, across and above the flickering water just a little ways up the hill from the area she had encircled. She pushed bushes and limbs with her eyes,

Canon followed them to the spot. The crackling of dried vegetation came to his ears, but nothing to his sight. He eased back into position, making himself still until he could place what he heard in his sights.

Mave could see what was in the brush in front of her, but the past memories began to blur her sight and pull her into a time she chose to forget. Her mind went back to the day she was not to go hunting with her father. She had hidden in the woods and watched him make the kill. That day was not like today, instead it was chilly with a noticeable bite to the air. The sun was up but didn't seem to shine so gloriously on that day. Mave's mother, she remembered, was upset with her father. They had been arguing the night before and again that morning about him going hunting and other things Mave didn't understand. She listened to her mother yelling at him about not wanting her the way he used to and just because she was crippled didn't mean she was dead. She told Mave she couldn't go with her father this time. It wasn't right, her being around him so much doing man things. So, Mave waited a while after her father left and her mother napped, then followed him to the area he hunted in. She smiled cleverly to herself about how surprised her father would be to see her and better than that, maybe she could spot his prey and kill it before him. Soon after she entered the area a shot went off about several yards from where she stood, just over a ridge. She stomped angrily with the realization he'd made the kill before she could. Then with the thought of helping him bring the kill home, her spirits picked up as she took to the ridge. She ran up the ridge stopping to pant for breath at the top. She could see him, but farther in the distance than the shot sounded. Mave saw clearly that the big man was her father. She could also see that the deer was a doe. Mave stood and watched her father. He was busying himself with the animal in a manner she never saw before. It was dead; she was sure. Not because it didn't move, but because he was a marksman and made shots only in the neck. He looked around, side to side. She ducked instantly. Finding a downed log two sizes the width of his arm and twice the length, he pulled it over to the kill. Taking the back hindquarters of the doe, he lifted the legs and pushed the log beneath it, right at the thighs. Mave didn't move. Nothing moved.

He took his left hand--the dominant, strongest, and smacked the meaty rump of the doe. She could hear him mumble a few words, then fumbled around in front of his body with both hands. A jingle sound carried on the wind to her ear, faintly. She knew it was his belt buckle that rattled. Then he fell to his knees. She saw his body then move in a slow graceful rhythm behind the animal, then picked up to a quick pace, rocking back and forth until he slumped in exhaustion. His arms flung out over the beast, and his cheek rested on the smooth flesh, smiling.

The loud sound of bushes rustling brought Mave back to the present and a stout buck came trotting, in the clearing. Canon raised his gun, glanced toward Mave, and aimed for behind the shoulder. This was a common shot made by hunters but would mean that the animal would not be killed right away and would have to be tracked until it fell from exhaustion or sickness. His gun was up as he positioned himself for the shot. Canon focused the sight on the barrel of the gun to his eye, almost ready. Boom! A sound exploded over his head and just as his finger squeezed the trigger. The buck collapsed without movement. Legs folded under, with head lying on top of the front legs: in prayer. Canon looked over at Mave pale, blank, and as a mist of smoke cleared, he could see the dark crown of hair around the soft features of his wife. The bleak empty sound and Canon's face were filled with Mave's voice:

"Looks like you got it. Clean, neck shot. I'll help you skin it if you show me how."

FIVE

Nathan

I walked into the daycare center dressed in high fashion. Stomach clenched against my H.L. Spencer silk and cotton slacks from dinner of pasta with baby zucchini in a red pepper sauce, croissants, and a Perrier water from the small town's hot little bistro. The glare of fluorescent lights blinding white when I entered the door and walked towards the kitchen. I lived thirty minutes outside of town and came into work at three a.m. Monday through Friday. I decided not to make the trip home since it was already late evening and instead go straight into work. I pulled up my satin sleeves, twisted on the hot water, and filled the sink with dishes and suds. One of the teachers appeared out of a room. I asked what she was still doing here. She said she was waiting for her husband to pick her up. It didn't ring clear to me until then that all of the lights were left on which possibly meant someone was still in the place. It was as though my biological sensors were tricked into reacting to the lights being on as normal because of the change I brought to the environment. I had come into the space unusually early and in an ill-suited attire so, to my defense, I didn't make anything of the lights being on. Then an unfamiliar male voice called from the floor above. The man's voice trailed after the sound of small feet that barreled down the stairs to the rhythm of the boy's name being called. "Nathan," the man's voice sang out spiritedly in the way Christmas stories are read. "Ok, you take the bucket and I've got the mop and broom and we're almost done."

My attention was pulled away from the sound of running feet and this man that told stories through the sound of his voice. I was now drawn to the teacher and her late-arriving husband, who entered loudly and full of late explanations. I moved from the sink to the counter that looked out into the dining area and wiped away crumbs and sticky rings of juice from the last snack of the day. I was in clear view of the couple standing just beyond the tables and near the entrance of the building. The husband seemed to stop and stare uneasily at me without changing the speed or timber of his speech. I wasn't sure what it was that warranted the disapproving look on his face; possibly my manner of dress did not fit what was expected of a cook or was it my blackness since he seemed fixated on my face. Whatever the reason, it was definitely a disapproving stare.

The couple finally headed out the door leaving me with a strange man, boy, and turkey rice soup to make. The remaining man darted past the kitchen, into the laundry room, and then across a sea of tables with benches architecturally aligned with the kitchen. His brown-rice-skinned colored little boy of six or seven with black-wolves hair and molasses-brown eyes ski-slid his feet with a slight bounce across the floor towards the room where the man was working. I watched his joy for a moment then glanced at my watch and knew I had to hustle if I wanted my coming in early to be worth it. So, I started a large package of turkey thighs to cook on the stove. I stuck the meat with a large fork and the dark meat was still tough and bled red from the punctures. I got a bowl and added flour, then baking powder, salt, and sugar weighed out from the scale of my hand. I sifted the ingredients, added eggs, butter, milk, and blueberries each in proper order. My eyes knew just how much it would take for thirty kids to receive one muffin each. Just as I stopped the whipping of the batter, the man appeared at the glassless picture window, where we served food during the school day. Startled, I jumped.

The man pointed to a plastic bag on the table, half filled with a caramel-colored cake. Cut into small squares with plump black raisins embedded in them. "I'm taking it for dog food," he said as if I might question it, which I did for a moment in my mind. I couldn't believe that it was for his dog. It looked neat and cleanly wrapped. I was sure there would have been other things he would have wanted to add from the trash if it was for the dog like the beans and weaners also served for lunch today.

"I took out the trash." He paused with a look, waiting for me to say something.

"That's fine, it doesn't affect me," I said. Then feeling as if I came off a little short in my tone, I quickly added, "So, you're the night man," trying to elevate his position of cleaning at night to some imagined position that still included taking out trash and cleaning.

"No, I just clean up at night," he said.

"Oh, I'm the cook, Ruth."

"I know. I met you that day I came in and thought you were Terri, the owner."

I didn't correct him, but I knew it wasn't me he met. It had to be the only other black person that worked here, a teacher who worked during the day. It seemed skin color and clothes caused a mistaken identity. He walked away and I moved slowly about the kitchen, having everything under control. I listened to him speak to the boy Nathan.

"Ok, Nathan, you take this and put it in my office."

"Office? Where dad? Where's your office?"

"In the closet in the restroom--I call that my office, Nathan."

His voice took on that singing ring especially when he said 'Nathan', which he said with each sentence as though it gave him pleasure to have the sound ring back into his ear. But what was surprising to me was not how much he said the boy's name, for even I enjoyed the way it toned from his mouth. Instead, it was the fact that the boy called him 'Dad' which jarred me. The man would have been a better Santa if he had the build for it rather than the wiry limbs he possessed. I say Santa because of the snow-white hair on top of his head and the caroling his speech made. Or maybe a recovered skid row bum because of the scraggly growth on his face and the quick hyper-movements he made. I was sure I could associate him with a bum or two I'd seen growing up. Most importantly, a grandfather, for he had to be in his late sixties. And even if he was this boy's father, they didn't even match. The boy had skin the color of black tea and milk and black raven's hair while the man was white. He spoke to Nathan again saying he'd have to mop now and then their conversation really started.

"Nathan, where do you live?"

"Where do I live, Dad?" Nathan replied. He answered, always with the same gentle singing.

"Yes, where do you live?"

"In Fairbanks."

"And what is the name of our state, Nathan?"

"Our state, Dad--what is it?

"Alaska, Nathan. Do you know what our capital's name is, Nathan?"

"Fairbanks, Dad."

"It's Juneau, Nathan. President Reagan is in Iceland right now with the Russian president Gorbachev. They're having a summit."

"What's the president's name, Dad?"

"Which president, Nathan?"

Nathan said nothing. I looked up and saw he had a puzzled look on his face.

"Nathan, do you know how many people are in the world?"

"No, Dad. How many...a billion?"

"There's over four billion, Nathan."

The old man had reached the doorway of my domain and said, "Do you mind if I go
ahead and mop in here? I won't make it real wet."

I said, "No, no, not at all. I hope I won't be in your way," making the point that I was here on his time, not mine, and was hoping he wouldn't complain to the owners. I think he suddenly realized that he had the upper hand when I said that, because of the way he paused and looked at me. But he chose not to use it against me.

"He just said, "No, you're not in my way. I just don't want you to slip and fall." Then he said with a smile, "Teaching my son a little political science."

I smiled and said, "You're teaching me a little, too." After I said that I felt so embarrassed like I broke some illusion he might have had of me.

He slung the mop sporadically over the floor. I thought of some of the teachers I heard one day I was picking up my check complaining about the way he cleaned. They said the owners got him because he bid the cheapest for the job, but that he doesn't do as much as the other people that used to clean. They now had to clean sinks and a list of other stuff that I didn't stay around to hear.

The man and boy went down the hall again, then dashed up the stairs for a moment. I took advantage of their absences and started on the snack: powdered milk, chunky peanut butter, raisins, honey, and rice crispies. I stirred the mixture with my hands, then started packing it into sheet pans so it could be cut into squares later. They both came back down the stairs.

I heard the old man say, "Ok, Nathan, I just have to vacuum, and we can go. I'll tell you what. Let's see if mom's home yet." The man dialed the phone on the wall and listened for a moment then handed the phone to Nathan and said, "You can talk to her while I work."

That was the first time I noted a drop or change in his voice. Nathan held the phone for what probably was two rings, then the old man said, "Not home. Well, we'll hang up. You can go do whatever you like."

Nathan got up and hopped around in one place for a few seconds like he hadn't moved for hours, then he asked, "Dad, what's the name of that place we went to that I liked?"

"Ah, what place, Nathan?

"You know, the one with the glacier."

"Oh, the Matanuska glaciers."

"Yeah, I like going there, Dad. I want to go there again."

They spoke loud over the vacuum that came to my end of the building again. The old man cut the vacuum off and took it upstairs. Nathan didn't follow this time but wandered around in front of the kitchen. I said to him, "Where's your favorite place in the whole world?" I was trying to get him to talk about the place he'd asked his dad about."

"School," he said.

I replied, "School?"

Then he said, "Home, I like staying home."

Seeing I was going to get nowhere I said, "What about that place you were asking your dad about?"

"Oh, Matanuska glaciers. There's this mo.., ah, raine we were standing on. One time this thing opened up and there was all this black mud. And if you fell down in it you couldn't get out. You'd be trapped. Once we fell in, but we got pulled out."

I stood agreeing with him saying, "Oh, yeah," not really understanding what he was talking about. I figured he wasn't sure of what certain things were called, like moraine? I'd never heard of such a thing.

Then he changed the subject and said, "I'm dad's helper. I wipe things for him. Who's your helper?"

I said I didn't have a helper, that I had to do it all by myself.

"Oh." he said, then turned and ran for the door saying, "Well, I got to go and help Dad."

The young boy was gone with his dad for four or five minutes when the two returned. The old man went down the hall and stood in the middle, wrapping the cord onto the vacuum.

"Nathan, turn out the lights."

A light went out on the opposite side of the door in the hallway. With movement quicker than I'd seen him move all evening, the old man rushed to where the light was out and turned it on again. My heart pumped for a moment, thinking he was angry with Nathan for making a mistake. But I had misconstrued his actions. Instead, his motives were much more simpler then some emotional charged or hidden trauma I believed was there. No, he was simply correcting a mistake that was made in his hyper movement way. The joyous sound of Nathan's name rang through, and his father directed him to where he wanted the lights turned out.

They came up to the counter where the mess from the snack I'd made, and still-hot blueberry muffins set cooling.

"We're going to leave now," the man said.

"Ok," I returned. He looked down at the food and my hands, still covered with some of the morsels of Rice Krispies and peanut butter.

"Are they going to have a party tomorrow?" the man asked.

"No, this is their snack."

A chunk fell from the side of the bowl. As I tried to wipe it free, he quickly moved for it without an ounce of hesitation.

"It's very good."

"Thank you."

"Here Nathan, I'll give you some, too." He found another chunk close to the bowl and placed it in Nathan's mouth. I wanted to offer them a muffin, but I couldn't get my mouth to say it.

"Do you give your dog turkey bones and stuff like that? Because if you do, I'll be glad to save some for you."

"Yes, I do. That would be fine, thank you."

"I'll put them in the freezer with your name on it. Now, what is your name?"

"Freedmont."

"I mean your first name."

"Freedmont. That's Freedmont Bryant."

They left. The building was quiet. I went to get the turkey I'd boiled earlier and placed it in a pan to cool in the freezer. I then tore the meat from the bones and removed the skin, cut the dark meat into small pieces, and placed it back in the stock that was left to reduce on the stove. I got a clean plastic bag from the drawer and put the bones and skin in. On the bag, I wrote 'Freedmont Bryant' and placed it close to the front, away from everything else so he wouldn't miss it.

———

SIX

Brother's Rain

She sat on the porch drinking Kool-Aid and soaking up the hot sun through her mulberry-colored skin. Her round belly sat up high in its eighth month. With each kick on the half-inch thick leather rind, a bead of sweat rolled off to the side and along a crease formed by her belly and thigh. It collected on her nylon pants sending the smell of talcum, synthetic, and unsexed odors to its maker.

Tammy sat watching the street: a mailman, a meterman, and two old ladies across the way working the earth in their gardens. They didn't seem alive like the kids at school, she thought, with radios screaming and pushing through the crowded restrooms for a drag of a cigarette or joint. Tammy sat watching the street in all its stillness she never knew existed in her fifteen years. She lived at home with her mother. Her brother, Ronnie, who hadn't been home for five years because of a prison sentence for armed robbery, used to live there too. He was fifteen at the time when he and friend, Tommy Rank, held up a liquor store. Tommy shot the man in the arm and left the scene. Because Ronnie was a minor, he went to juvenile detention. He also had a previous record of breaking and entering and shoplifting. When he turned legal age eighteen, he stood trial and was sentenced to three years in prison.

Tammy got up from her seat of sweat, lifting herself by pressing her fists into the cushions of the chair. Her fragile wrists were like breadsticks, thin and brown, they cracked and crunched from the weight. She swayed from one side then to the other towards the bathroom. Removing her underwear, she washed, dried, and powdered her privates and replaced the nylon panties with a new pair. She went into the kitchen. The counter was lined with morning dishes. An old white gas stove top was speckled with bacon fat. A black skillet sat, pooling with drippings and bits of soft fat, that had sizzled itself a golden brown in the cooling hot oil. Tammy picked up the fat gently, like a fine crystal stemware, and shook it lightly. The excess grease coated her nails like a clear lacquer. The pigment where the skin and nail met was black like the skillet, leaving the nail to seem separate from the finger and float in the shiny pool of grease. She placed the two fingers in her mouth and the taste of salt and a sweet, smokey flavor oiled her tongue. Then sucking the last bits from her fingers and nails, a sweet taste came like the smell of baby powder and bitter (like soap). She turned the tap and swished water about trying to remove the taste.

The phone rang. Chewing an apple quickly, she held the receiver, then swallowed and said, "Errumph...hello,"

"Tammy, Mama-- I'm going to be home late. I have to pick up a few things from the store. You need anything?"

"No Mama. Ohh we're out of Kool-Aid."

"I know, I see you used the last package last night. You drink that stuff like it's going out of style. Try drinking plain water or milk. That's more better for the baby than Kool-Aid. Alright, I'll see you, and clean up that kitchen before I get home."

Tammy turned on the television and headed for the kitchen. A roast pan sat on the counter soaking from last night's meat and the yolks of breakfast eggs dried to a lucid yellow on stacked dishes. She rattled the dishes, pushing them to one side, then plugged the sink.

Thoughts of what her mother said reminded her of her pregnancy which she stopped thinking about long ago. She stopped thinking about it right after she told her mother and got a beating, after her boyfriend stopped coming around and right after her stomach got large enough to say she was pregnant and not just gaining weight. She pretended to herself that she was just expelled from school, and soon would be back bullshitting with the rest of them. The sun was high and shone hot through the kitchen window over the sink and hit her ripening belly. A foot stuck under Tammy's small ribs, rendering her in pain and unable to move. She pressed hard on the area and called to the person inside, "Move baby, you're hurting me." She gave another hard press and a, "Please move." She gripped the sink and pools started to form in her eyes. The pain slowly subsided, and a cloud rolled in front of the sun. As the shade cooled her belly, she thought of what she might name the person inside.

The phone rang just as she finished her last dish and released the dish water.

"Hello."

"Yeah, Tammy what you doing, kid? This is your brother."

"Ronnie, what's happening, big bro. Why you haven't called in months, turkey?"

"Ah, been busy. You know how it is."

"What can you be busy doing in there--making license plates?"

"Don't be smart. They don't make license plates anymore. So how's the little Mama and my niece or nephew doin'?"

"We alright. I only got another month to go."

"Speaking of months, guess what? I'm getting out in another month, maybe a week or two earlier, good behavior."

"Hey, you might be here to see the baby born."

"Yeah, tell Mama. I got to go now."

"See ya Ronnie. I love you."

"Me too, little sister."

The weeks passed and school was letting out. Some of the high school kids were wandering around the streets. Tammy sat looking out the window over the porch, occasionally giving a yell to someone and an invitation to call. A tall, thin girl in bright yellow shorts started up the walk. Tammy flew out of the door like she was running to a lover in a foreign movie. She stopped when they got up to each other and slapped hands saying, "What's happening, girl?" They sat on the concrete stairs and watched the late comers straggle from school.

"Tammy, there's that bitch I was telling you about that's been hanging around Derrick. Her girlfriend's been messing with Mark."

"Let's Jack with them," the thin girl said.

They walked down onto the sidewalk and made comments out loud.

"I hear the bitch in the red shorts gave him gonorrhea."

"Well, I'm glad I ain't doin' him no more. He might give the baby somethin'."

"I heard they were trying to get pregnant but Derrick told the bitches they're too ugly to have his babies. The only ones ever going to have his and Mark's babies were me and you…. Roll your eyes bitch, I bet you won't come over here and do that."

"Ah, forget them. Let's go up on the porch."

"How much longer before the baby's born?"

"Suppose to be another week."

"You talk to Derrick? He coming to the hospital?"

"I don't know--when he found out it was too late to have an abortion, he quit callin'. Mama told me not to be beggin' like no dog for him, to do right; that it's my responsibility now since I got myself in trouble. So I ain't called him no more."

"Hey, there's your brother Ronnie!"

"Where?"

"Over there, coming down the street. I didn't know he was out?"

"Ronnie!" Tammy screamed, rushed down to meet him as quick as she could.

They got up on the porch and he looked at Tammy's girlfriend and said, "Damn girl, you filled out real nice."

"Ronnie," Tammy said nudging him. "That's all y'all think about."

She blushed and told Tammy she'd see her tomorrow. They went into the house and Tammy smothered him with questions, none of which he wanted to answer. He changed the subject to his mother.

"How's Mama doing?"

"She's alright. She don't talk much to me no more."

"She still mad about me and you getting into trouble?"

"Yeah, she just look at me blank and if I talk about you she's blank too."

"I got to make it up to Mama, all we done put her through. I got a trade when I was in the joint doing books, accounting work. I'm going to see if I can get a part-time job doing books and go to school the rest of the time."

"How you get into trouble anyway.? You were real smart in school. Had the best grades. Everybody thought you would be the first valedictorian," Tammy said in a pondering voice.

He answered back, "Yeah, I know, but I could ask you the same thing. You were pretty smart too, I guess we were just too smart for our own good."

"After I have the baby I want to finish school and go into nursing."

"That's the way to think little sister, up and out," Ronnie said smiling.

Their mother walked in the door and placed her sacks on the chair without even noticing her son sitting in the chair across from her. She straightened up and took a step towards the kitchen. When she saw him, a small shine came to the corner of her mouth. Tammy looked on pleased that her mother seemed happy to see him and wondered what was going through her mind. But the shine faded, and her mother's eyes glared at the full-grown man of twenty that stood in front of her with faded green army fatigues and a sweatshirt that was too small.

"Hi, Mama."

"I see they let you out a little early."

"Yeah, I have to see a parole officer once a month."

"What's your plans?"

"Well, I'd like to stay here; I'm going to look for work tomorrow. I got a trade when I was in there."

"Doin' what?" she said skeptically.

"Bookkeeping, I want to work part-time and go to college."

"How you gonna do that? You didn't even finish school before you got into that mess."

Slightly irritated with his mother's lack of enthusiasm over him being home and his accomplishments while away, he held his tongue and proceeded to explain, "I didn't want to tell Tammy. I wanted it to be a surprise. I got my GED. It's the same as a diploma."

"Same," his mother scoffed.

"Mama, I'm trying! Give me a chance! I know I've made mistakes and hurt you, but I'm going to make it up now."

She didn't say much but told him if he was going to stay, he was going to have to find some kind of work. She couldn't support all of them.

....

Two weeks passed and Tammy hadn't delivered and neither did Ronnie. Everywhere he applied, they turned him down. "Not enough experience," they told him after he said he had a record. Ronnie was beginning to stay home less and less and was never around when his mother was there. During the day, Tammy and Ronnie would sit and stare blankly with the T.V. or radio, or both. She sat rubbing the lump in front of her, breathing shallow, wanting it over, and wondering how much it would hurt.

Ronnie sat in a chair opposite her, looking like a tree at the end of fall when its sap sank to the bottom. Earlier that day, a friend of his told him about a burglary he was going to do. His friend said to meet him on the corner of 48th & Main, across from the liquor store, tonight. Ronnie shook his head and said, "No" out loud to himself and then, "Damn it, somebody's got to give me a job!"

Tammy tried consoling him by saying, "You'll get something," and then telling him about a help-wanted sign she saw at McDonald's. He looked at her. They both laughed and he said, "Could you see me dressed in those funny-looking suits. Looking like one of them damn Big Macs."

"Ronnie, if it's a boy, I want to name it after you."

"For what? I ain't dead."

"I know that."

"I was just kidding. I like that, a little Ronnie Jr. - yeah, the second, that's cool."

Their mother came in at 6:30 that evening and Ronnie laid in the back room on the bed while Tammy cooked in the kitchen. The sky was darkening with clouds. It had turned a color that wasn't a blue now or a gray or white. Tammy went over to the sink and stared at the sky trying to understand what color it was, to give it a name. Although she saw this color many times before, she needed to name it this time. She heard her mother and brother arguing, and then the door slammed, and her mother appeared in the kitchen.

"What you cooking?"

"Chicken."

A light rain began to fall, and the sound mingled with the skin on the chicken frying like someone hushing you in a low voice. Tammy felt something wet between her legs and went to the bathroom. She sat on the toilet and felt a relief when her water ran out, but it didn't last long like a normal urination for her those days. She wiped and noticed an orange-like color. She heard her brother come out of the room and slam the door. She ignored the red-orange water in the stool, pulled up her pants, wet her fingers under the tap and rushed out. He was at the door and their mother was standing next to him. Tammy could hear the rain from the opened door coming down slightly harder.

Her mother was saying, "Ronnie don't be silly. Where you gonna go, it's starting to rain like something crazy. I didn't say you had to get out, I just said you needed to take a job. Anything until you can do better."

"I don't want anything. I worked hard to be a bookkeeper in the joint and that's what I want, or I'll go to hell first!" Ronnie's voice clapped like thunder.

"Ronnie, come in here!" The mother yelled after him.

Tammy stood in the middle of the floor. The sound of the rain began to pound in her ears, though it could hardly be heard by any others if they were in the house. The baby made no movement. Her mother came away from the door and went into her room and closed the door behind her. Tammy went into the kitchen and finished frying the chicken, placed it on a platter, covered it with foil and stuck it in the warm oven. She went to her brother's room. The single bed was wrinkled from him lying on it. The closet was open and bare except for a few things her mother stored there. Tammy laid on the bed trying to get in his exact imprint. She could feel the warmth of his body. She sunk deep into the mattress and then she fell asleep.

She awoke to the room in total darkness. The rain had calmed back down to a light sprinkle. Her pelvis and the pit of her stomach ached with cramps; like menstruation cramps she thought, but deeper. She then remembered the toilet and wondered if that was her water breaking. It couldn't be, she thought. There's supposed to be a flood of it, wetting everything. Then the dream came to her.

She sat up fast and a sharp grip came in her stomach. Instead of just cramps, these were pains. She lay there waiting for the pain to stop as the sound of the rain began to fall heavier. She started remembering the dream. A boy was on the corner under a light. No, by a building with a light on it. He stood in the doorway. Everything was dark around him except the light above his head. She could hear him arguing with someone. He kept saying, "No," and something else, but the rain was too loud for her to hear what he said.

"Au!" Tammy cried deep in her throat when the pain hit her again, harder this time. She thought of calling out for her mother, but it hurt too bad. She would wait till the pain stopped. She began to wonder if she called out, would her mother hear her over the rain? It was beating harder now, and the wind was swaying the trees. The leaves rattled like gold chains.

She thought maybe her brother was in the living room with her mother watching T.V. She had forgotten to call out, then the pain struck her again. She curled up tight in a knot and grunted, "Oh God, help me." A breeze blew through a cracked window and sent the blinds fluttering like a baseball card flapping against the spoked of a bike tire. She then laid still, waiting for the pain to leave. The thought of the dream came again. "What if it meant death?" she thought. The sound of voices interrupted; it was only the T.V. from the other room. The dream was in her mind, like the pain and the rain outside, coming back and forth. She saw a person, a boy, lying on the ground and the rainwater washing his blood down the dark street. Then, "Mama!" she screamed, loud and strong. Her mother flung open the door. A golden light from the living room shone behind her dark figure.

"Tammy, what is it?"

Tammy said in a high-pitched strain, "Pain, Mama. This time it's not going away."

"Why didn't you call me? Never mind that now. I'll call an ambulance."

She rushed out, then came right back. She turned on the bright ceiling light. Tammy turned away, then balled up screaming in pain. "Mama, help me!" The rain splattered hard on the window and the wind pushed the wooden slat of the blind against the windows to a click, click clock beat. Her mother turned her over and propped her back with pillows.

"Is it coming all the time now?"

"Yes," Tammy said, then she turned to ask her mother about Ronnie. All she could say was his name.

Her mother answered, "Don't be worrying about him now, you concentrate on having the baby."

Her mother ran and got some clean towels, took off Tammy's pants, then told her when the pain came again to come up and push hard like she's having a bowel movement. A knock came to the front door. Her mother yelled for them to come on in. Tammy asked if it was Ronnie. Her mother told her no, that it was probably old lady Henderson. She had called her, too. The pain hit just as Mrs. Henderson graced the door.

Mrs. Henderson asked Tammy's mother, "Is the baby down?"

Her mother answered, "I can see the head." Then she said, "Where the hell's the ambulance?"

Mrs. Henderson said, "Don't worry about that now. Baby be here before they will. She told Mama to go and get some water and something to suck the baby's mouth out. The pain hit again.

Mrs. Henderson said, "O.k. Chil', push!"

"I can't push no more," Tammy said raspily.

"You better push. Less you want your brother to walk in on you like this."

Tammy pushed and pushed and thought of dying, then pushed some more. She wanted to cry but couldn't because she was too busy pushing and thinking of death. Then silence. The rain was not there, nor the pain, or her thinking of death. Tammy could hear a siren outside, and the slushing sound of the baby being suctioned out. Then a cry, a loud deep cry, and a voice saying, "It's a boy."

The paramedics carried Tammy and the baby on a stretcher into the ambulance. The tarred street was shining beneath the streetlight and the water beaded on the black oily surface. Tammy felt clean with the smell of water on the wind. While placing her in the ambulance, a voice came over the radio. "213, we have a stabbing of a black male around 20, 25 on 48th and Main. Police are already on the scene; need transport. No emergency, already DOA."

The End

About the Author

Olivia Hill shares her journey of mental health, literacy, and being a Black woman within the creative arts to many audiences. She is a published short-story author and playwright of over five plays that have been produced in multiple states. She is the recipient of the Lorraine Hansberry Award for her play *Mother Spense*.

As a visual artist, she has specialized in printmaking and watercolor, exhibiting in multiple galleries.

Hill attended culinary school early in her educational career, later becoming an entrepreneur and starting Solomon's Rose, a gourmet food company and catering business. She ran her company for over thirteen years and sold products throughout the East Coast.

Hill holds a Bachelor of Arts in Theater from the University of Alaska Fairbanks. She resides back in her hometown, Kansas City, Missouri, where she continues to be an activist on social issues that affect BIPOC creatives and love on her grandchildren.

Acknowledgments

Front cover design and format editing by Diane Swanson.
Images from Shutterstock.
Fonts include: *KG Dancin' on the Rooftop, Humble Cafe, KG Life is Messy, Oswald* and *American Typewriter Regular.*

WORKS BY OLIVIA HILL
Available for download at
www.oliviahillwrites.com:

Made in USA - Kendallville, IN
84176_9798841285755
09.01.2022 1606